T0065314

ENI
& Other Poems

Ekpe Inyang

Langaa Research & Publishing CIG
Mankon, Bamenda

Publisher:
Langaa RPCIG
Langaa Research & Publishing Common Initiative Group
P.O. Box 902 Mankon
Bamenda
North West Region
Cameroon
Langaagrp@gmail.com
www.langaa-rpcig.net

Distributed in and outside N. America by African Books Collective
orders@africanbookscollective.com
www.africanbookscollective.com

ISBN-10: 9956-762-69-5

ISBN-13: 978-9956-762-69-9

© Ekpe Inyang 2017

All rights reserved.
No part of this book may be reproduced or transmitted in any form or by
any means, mechanical or electronic, including photocopying and
recording, or be stored in any information storage or retrieval system,
without written permission from the publisher

DISCLAIMER
All views expressed in this publication are those of the author and do not
necessarily reflect the views of Langaa RPCIG.

Table of Contents

Digital smile
22 March 2016

We now live in the digital age
This everyone surely knows
Where nearly everything is rendered digital
But never crossed my mind it could also include a smile

Everyone sings and dances to digital music
Issuing from digital radios, televisions or high-tech sets
Surely no need for guitarists, drummers, pianists, trumpeters
Each lacking the touch of digital sound albeit wearing a
digital smile

Beautiful Sunshine

27 April 2016

Beautiful, beautiful, beautiful, beautiful
When at last Day raises her curtain
To display but soft, soothing sunshine
Beautiful, beautiful, beautiful, indeed
Beautiful, beautiful, beautiful, beautiful
In the baking-hot seaside city of Limbe
Where Fako's skirt soaks in Atlantic
Beautiful, beautiful, beautiful, indeed

Beautiful, beautiful, beautiful, beautiful
On the Atlantic Coast of Cameroon
Sun now sooths the smooth dark skin of beauty
Beautiful, beautiful, beautiful, indeed

Can Be Reversed

1 July 2016

Early and dearly in deepening thoughts
Sat I up in bed at dawn contemplating
Changes occurring too swift to comprehend
Inviting some disturbing moments
Loading a billion hearts with icy melancholy
Uncertainty colouring the sail of life
But I denounce that weird picture
In unprecedented conviction that
With determined hope and verve can reverse
Events surely more malignant and catastrophic

Carrying Papers
6 January 2016

He was born in ComeAlone
A country on earth
Which makes him a global citizen
Supposedly free to travel
From West to East
And from South to North
Without restraint

But each time he travels
Even within ComeAlone
He is required
To carry papers to show
As proof of nationality
A man who travelled to earth
Without a paper

Obliged to travel on earth
Carrying papers
That often expire
And must be renewed
To permit him travel on earth when
On leaving earth back to where he came
He will need no such papers

Change Climate Change

2 March 2016

Apply
With rigour
Polluters Pay Principle
Increase awareness
The storms are raging
Icecaps are melting
The seas are rising
Species are threatened
Send down the hammer
Cut down emissions
Reduce consumption
Switch to eco-technologies
Fade out your eco-footprints
Wake up to a bright new day
Help write the global anthem
Sing a new song for Mother Earth
Put out your lights in collective action
Join the fight to change climate change

Christmas

30 December 2015

Gold now permeating
The clear blue above
In awesome dominance
Millions of eyes dazzled, squinting
Unable to fix steady gazes
Colourful rays too strong to permit

And now and then chirping
Thrilling sounds from thick bushes
Marking journey to great carnival
Eagles soaring over wondrous canopies
Green, white, purple, yellow, red
Prodigious skyline to the sight

Cold Network
2 October 2015

Network growing old
I seem to be told

So, so cold
With no supplier of the coal

Are the few left not that bold
For all to uphold?

King Of Forest
27 May 2015

Listen to the horn sound
The quickening of steps
As everyone longs to be part
Of the great event
The crowing of King of Forest

Birds stop chirping
Rivers cease flowing
The wind stops blowing
The sun goes to bed
Flowers bowing as he makes an entrance

A great ceremony it promises to be
From the look of things
A stool fashioned from gold
Placed at the centre, surrounded by singers, surrounded yet
By hundreds of heads with enough to eat and drink

Sounds of music
Sounds of hailing
Sounds of dancing steps
Sounds of plates and bottles embracing
Sounds so sweet and so-o-o-o...sweet

Doesn't Serve Him Right

1 August 2014

Looking for the light
He climbed up a height
Picked a new sight
Went for a hike
Received a bite
When he saw a kite
Which took a flight
 To the sky bright
Doesn't serve him right

Embracing the Night
17 May 2016

She dashed out of the kiosk
Wearing a strong musk
Flaunting the might of her lone tusk
Looking so brusque
Still poised to embrace the dusk

She knew it's not that easy
Braving weather so breezy
Manned by insane guys busy
Throwing words quite cheesy
Causing sane minds so dizzy

Though often she was always right
That lone night she could hardly write
Home about anything but fright
She's sure not ready anymore to fight
As she'd speedily lost her lone might

Eni
(In memory of my beloved wife)

Once Ever Near Inyang, now Never Near Inyang
I feel like pouring my tears on Facebook, not to wet it
I feel like mourning you to the whole wide world, not to
shock it
As the storm in me gallops and tumbles like a wild jungle
river

Eni, the wife that was given to me by He that is on High
The wife I received, with all my heart, on my knees, with both
hands
The wife I thought would spend all of her life with me
All of her life I calculated to be so long enough to see our
children's children

As was the song on that day when a ring I gave you and you
gave me
But you took that sudden exit on 1 November 2014, sharing
no clear word with me
Which plunges me into speechlessness, hopelessness,
helplessness!!!!!!!!
Your early exit leaves me hollow like an empty cave in a
lifeless forest

What shall I now do with the remaining part of my life
without you?
How do I take care of myself without you?
How do I bring up the children without you?
Has fate succeeded to twist our life's straight story?

Eni, Ever Near Inyang, but now Never Near Inyang
Take this as my last pouring ("I hope so") on your palms that
sure still burn with love
May joy take its place as you intercede for grace to complete
our life's project
Just as you now take on the greater assignment from He that
gave me you

Enjoy the Song
5 August 2016

Enjoy the song
Sitting in the sun
As it's sweetly sung
By your dandy son

Hear the gong
Played by a Dun
Sitting on the dung
Waiting for a Don

Fake Trumpet-sound

23 May 2015

Round and round
Goes the fake sound
In acquiescent town

Going down
To kiosk they had no bound
To get a pound

To fetch a gown
And a crown
To dress the clown

Special mission-bound
To spread round
Fake trumpet-sound

Global warming
19 April 2016

Carbon Dioxide?
Yes, my Lord, Carbon Dioxide is the lead actor
Ensuing from burning of fossil fuels
Running cars, lorries, generators, okadas and all
Not to mention industries and factories
With towering chimneys

Centres for producing products for our wants and needs
Even kitchens where cooking is done with biomass fuels
Daily to fill millions of stomachs
And come to think of diminishing forests
Whose trees would have been sucking up the excess in
atmosphere
To reduce the thickness of the heat-trapping blanket

Water Vapour, Methane, Nitrous Oxide, and Ozone in
troposphere,
My Lord, appearing there in so much smaller quantities
Should not be brought under the same weight of international
justice
Though collectively they form the blanket that envelops the
earth
Trapping and sending heat that would have escaped into
space
Back to warm the earth again and again, causing global
warming

Goteborg
29 June 2015

Goteborg
Seen through
An eye from Gothia Towers
Beautiful streets
Houses, hotels, restaurants
Green spaces, lawns, crossings
Relaxation parks, night clubs

Goteborg
Sensed from short walks in nearby streets
Sweet smells, nice foods, great music
Inviting air (not weather!) and people
Everything reminiscent of Scotland's
Glasgow 1990, European City of Culture

Having Drained His Glass

8 June 2016

Nara X thought he had
Emptied the glass
Bara had filled for himself
Over many long years'
Toil and pain and pay
Since Bara had dished out to him
So generously
Seemingly unreservedly

Now Nara X prides himself
He surely can dish out
As much as Bara but would dare not
Give it all to others and get
Thrown off that pride of place
As now he feels he can
Quietly take Bara's place
Having drained his glass

Nara X's now so bold
Arrogant best describes him
He feels he can let the ink flow
Like Bara does paint with ease the pages
With scintillating colours of wisdom
Having drained Bara's glass
That raised simple Bara to genius
Renowned and revered by all

How I Use My Break Time
2 October 2015

Staring at the ceiling
Dozing on the chair

Eating Fufu and Eru
Downing a beer

Gossiping with friends
Swapping reminiscences

Incompatible Blend
29 December 2015

High and mighty, haughty
Most grandiloquent
Short syllabic utterances
Sombrely rendered
Such torrential cascades
Expressing ferocity and magnanimity
Fine blend of sugar and vinegar

Riches of Kenya

15 May, 2016

The Great Rift Valley
Blinding beauty, rolling splendour
Making you giddy

Lake Naivasha
Teaming with terrestrial wildlife
Not beating aquatic lifeforms

Hell's Gate National Park
Nature's unrivaled architecture
Crafting scenes of unmatched standards
Site of international film-making

Nairobi National Park
Warehouse of wild wonders
Impala, zebra, giraffe, ostrich, crocodile, lion…

The Animal Orphanage
Inviting you to show your utmost care
Adding value to nature's gifts

Go Get It

30 June 2016

Go get it
It's something worth going for
What you have stored in your head
Is worth more than what you've hidden in your pocket

Pursue it with all your might
It's something worth fighting for
What you have stored in your head
Is worth more than what you've hidden under your pillow

Go get it
It's something worth taking the pains to achieve
What you have stored in your head
Is worth more than what you have hidden in your safe

Pursue it with all your might
For it can be carried West, East, North and South
Converted into cash at will
And no thief can rob you of it

Lies and Truth

28 April 2016

Lies are a team of millions
But weak to the bone
Cos they are of man
Master of injustice
Truth a team of one
But strong to the marrow
Cos it is of God
Lord of justice

Light Is Truth
2 October 2015

Light travels
Sun to Earth
Piercing through
Thickness of space
Passing through
Length of time
Reaches Earth
In all its colours
Hence Truth
No matter how long
Twisted before
Or hidden from eyes and ears
Will surely egg-hatch
Revealing the chick in its naked form
All elements intact
To shape views
And transform landscapes
Seascapes
Egoscapes
And anthroposcapes
Justice and peace seizing the palace

Little by little

2 October 2015

Little by little
The chick keeps growing
From an egg
Into a wingless chick fed by its mum
Then into a chick with feeble wings still fed by its mum
Then into a chick with wings
Strong enough to help it fly about
Looking for its own food

Messily
9 August 2016

The daystarteddrowsily
Waking us up noisily
Couldn't sit up easily
To get on busily
As it tumbled messily

On A Hard Rock Of Regrets

20 August 2015

You abandoned your partner, your bosom friend
On this parched lump of dust
Trapped alone to bear the sudden
Surge of scorching heat you both envisaged
A stream of coarse acidic dust that now bruises his being

Ignorantly, you loaded his fertile soil of vibrant life
With fat cankerworms of blind egocentricity
That has sucked up every tiny drop of life-supporting
moisture
Leaving behind a sullen trail of acidic dust covering
And corroding the lens of the vision you shared with him

You assembled what you saw as earthworms
Filial strands that would serve to enrich your soil of common
hope
And create a substrate on which your seedlings would surely
also grow
But which ended up emitting a huge cesspool of acidic dust
That swiftly corroded you into nothingness for their longing
gain

Parched earth, cesspool of acidic dust now his source of pain
Substrates that are no support for growth of the seedlings left
to his lone care
But a huge source of stress that threatens the foundation you
both built

What a reward for your strong, unending filial props – spirit of ingratitude, out!
Footprints of sacrifices clearly engraved on a hard rock of regrets

Ozone
18 April 2016

Ozone
Produced within the tropics
Forming a thick layer over the far reaches of Mother Earth
High, high up in stratosphere

Such a huge umbrella over Mother Earth
Protecting her and all lifeforms
Including humans of all civilizations
In North, in South, in East, in West from
Destruction by ultraviolet rays

Ozone
Such a friend when far, far away
But an abrasive enemy when close to Mother Earth
When your molecules are found in troposphere

Your presence in troposphere
Detected by humans with good sense of smell
Or by rapid corrosion of earthly materials
Car tyres wearing faster than normal
Or some peculiar health problems

Ozone
 Surely you also are destroyed as humans
Use fire extinguishers, refrigerators, aaerosol sprays hiding in
Chlorofluorocarbons whose single chlorine atom when
released

Destroy thousands of your molecules in one catalytic reaction
Causing a hole in your protective stratospheric layer
Making Mother Earth and all lifeforms threatened
As a single stream of ultraviolet rays
May cause more than humans now estimate

Rise and Walk

12 August 2016

If life were simply rise and walk
Success not meaning bend and work
And the sun shining east to west
Giving us enough time to rest
We shall our tools store up in room
And still be sure to have a boom

But since it comes with streams of sweat
Our tools we must all bear in duet
Leisure and luxury give no mark
Hence we must ensure there's a bark
That serves as store for future use
As we all cast our various dues

Round and Round

14 September 2015

Round and round
The Earth moves on its axis
And the night gives way to day
Round and round
The Earth moves on its orbit
And the seasons come and go

As the earth moves round and round
So does your life move round and round
Bringing in moments of sorrow and of joy
Moments of poor health and of good health
Moments of want and of plenty
Times you are down and times you are up

Until the Earth ceases to move
Round and round on its axis and orbit
Then will life remain ever the same
Each moment brings in its own peculiar taste
Good or bad receive with thanks
As each carries its own bundle of favours

Sandskär
3 July 2015

Pictures and images of dozens of tourists
Some fresh from Saunas, looking refreshed
Others at breakfast, lunch or dinner, celebrating rich Swedish menu
Then of seals applauding the Baltic writing wavy notes of splendid music
And of islands like stars in this heavily salted sea shared also with Finland
But one stands out really bold, beckoning every visitor like Ajita from India
Marvelled, I said to Staffan
Take me there to dine with Nature, kiss the seals and taste the salmons
But just how this could happen
We couldn't figure out
Year after year
We couldn't decide how and when
Then came World Environmental Education Congress 2015
But who will foot the bills for Ekpe?
So much haze in the sky
Then suddenly an email
Germund had the answer
WWF Sweden happily will
Then Ekpe must visit me
He must breathe Haparanda in Beautiful North
Staffan was more than happy
Accommodating me for days

Summer House of Leif my Palace on Sandskär
Gradually, gradually, Dream has birthed Reality
Visa to flight and train tickets to hotel bills, WWF Sweden paid
Douala to Istanbul, Istanbul to Goteborg
Rich, inspiring WEEC over, Goteborg to Stockholm by train
With Germund and Gunilla, then, Stockholm to Lulea
There met and picked by wife and friend of Staffan, Lena
To Haparanda City where now the Sun smiles 24 hours
Alas, the man! Chief Ranger, Ecotourism Entrepreneur
ESD Consultant, Staffan, rushing from his boat, Bosmina
Bigger than the moose and smarter than the goose
Kinder than the reindeer and cleverer than the fox
Baltic animals common in this beautiful, terrific
Cold, warm, cold, warm island of Sandskär

Seeing The Light

16 May 2015

When man shall learn
To mend his ways
And every tongue
Spits more of love
And every heart
Beats more of peace
And every hand
Shows more of care
And every step
Points more to right
And every season's
Bounteous fruit's
Everybody's
Fair share of life
Know every eye
Sees more the light

S-FAN
27 April 2016

Back from the field
Great teachers to support
Task not as easy
As report does convey
Muscles now sore
Back-stopping work so arduous
But mind so strong
And heart so joyous
For surely it is clear
Model lessons are born
From every single school subject
Writing ESD anthem
To support LORETs teaching
Locally Relevant Themes
Addressing local challenges
To make education relevant
Raising the flag of ESD
Singing sustainability
Education for Sustainable Development
Sustainability Fan for All Nations

Siting on the grass

9 August 2015

Siting on the grass
Drinking from a glass
Listening to the brass
Watching at the lass
Dancing to the jazz

Soaked in Selfishness
12 May 2016

Sackcloth of society
Soaked in selfishness
Sulkiness, sliminess
Sluggishness, sheepishness
Stinginess, sickliness
Silliness, slipperiness
Sneakiness, slyness
Sarcasm, sadism

Sonnet of Nature Walk

12 March 2015

It was terribly scorching
But I set off for a walk
Stubborn as I am
Through a glade so scary
Picking a path snaky
Exuding sweat real sticky
Panting like a dog utterly thirsty
Trudging like a cockroach long, long sick
Then came the breeze gusty
And I felt so refreshed
The air now sweetly scented
Flowers on both sides brightly coloured
Waiving in patterns mesmerizing
Ushering me to the kingdom of floral beauty

Staffan Svanberg

(In memory of a great friend
and brother from Sweden)
3 May 2016

Stands distinguished
Tall amongst giants in any business his hand holds
Animator in ESD, boat driving, tour guiding, nature
interpretation
Full of bubblingenergy and enthusiasm
Fan of fun to kill the surging stress of life
Always digging up jokes to share
Never tired of finding new ways to serve you happiness

Succinctly talks of Mongolia, India, Africa, especially
Cameroon
Very passionate in his dealing with people, spreading ESD
seeds
Amiably, amicably, amenably, admirably
Notable distinguished amongst notables in Sandskär,
surprisingly
Bosmina's final destination on tour missions
Effortlessly hospitable, magnanimous, benevolent
Reluctant to say
Goodbye to visitors from far and near

The Danger of a Single Story

24 September 2015

You've been going around saying that…
And I have decided that…
The danger of a single story

You have been carrying out…
And have caused this problem of…
The danger of a single story

You have refused to…
And have stagnated our…
The danger of a single story

You are known to be…
And that is why I cannot…
The danger of a single story

The Razor
22 April 2016

Who invented the razor
Encoded a message
Too complex to decode

Then I saw a jumping razor
Playing the invented razor
And I got the message right

I used to tell the twins
Don't toy with a razor
And for the third time
They learnt the lesson right

With this edge it cut the boy
With the other it nicked the girl
What a sharp scream both did give

Don't toy with a razor
Watch out for edges doubled
Don't toy with a razor

The sky

26 January

The sky is known by the colour of blue
Yet you see the dark and the gray
Patches that form a good part of it
Life is meant to be lived to the fullest
Dressed in abundance, health, comfort, joy

Time To Stitch

24 May 2015

I sense an itch
It's time to stitch
Evade the hitch
The gory pitch
The gaping ditch
The fangs of bitch
Belly of witch

Beware Quick Conclusions
15 April 2016

The dog barks in front of the house
The fox sneezes near the pig sty behind
The lizard nods its head on the wall in the living room
Guess, what's going on?

The cock crows atop the house roof
The guinea fowl cackles in the bush
The lizard nods its head on the wall in the living room
Guess, what's really going on?

The pussy cat pews under the table
The lion roars in its den in the wild
The lizard nods its head on the wall in the living room
What next is your conclusion?

So down-to-earth

19 July 2016

Finally he met the man
And asked curiously,
"Why are you so down-to-earth?"
And the man said subconsciously,
"I am made from dust of earth,
"Logically live on dust,
"Grow on earth,
"Stand on earth,
"Walk the earth,
"Work on earth,
"Sleep on earth,
"Wake on earth
"Live on earth,
"The vessel that races on
"Faster than the fastest rocket,
"But which never makes me giddy
"To give me fear of falling off
"Even for a moment,
"Except that man stirs up wars,
"Instilling endless fear and stress
"To break the hearts of fellow men."

Will There Ever Be Change?
14 May 2016

Will there ever be change
When most youngsters still buy papers
Earn high marks while those that toil
Earn lower marks but carry in them knowledge and skills
Across the subjects
Pass job-oriented exams with ease
When it comes to the written part
But fail the orals year-after-year like tired horses
Galloping over rough terrain 'cos they can't speak
The language of the landscape
Like those guys with high marks in subjects they can't spell
Will there ever be change?

Will there ever be change
When most of them proudly flag their licenses
With sumptuous rides of Pajeros, Pathfiners, Prados
Glad they're the smarter guys
Topping the world with what matter most while
Those that topped the class
Sprawl around like Nebuchadnezzars
Flanking the streets waiting for cabs
Asking for lifts or begging for alms
But inspiring the crowds with polished language
Churning out ideas that earn no pay
Will there ever be change?

Will there ever be change
When those that swindle
Gain new heights
Competing with coconut
Trees much taller
Than those once loftier
But now made shorter
'Cos they dared to say
The truth so bitter
Painting faces of faceless Goliaths
Grave offence exposing fraudsters
Will there ever be change?

Will there ever be change
When the river between
The rich and the poor
Widens daily, no ferry afloat
When the hungry
Can't afford tiny meals
Most days of each new month
When many a lad spends
Honeymoon nights under bridges
Perching with new friends each new month
Knocking door to door
Will there ever be change?

Will there ever be change
When those in power
Get craftily recycled
In lands without
Such green industries
But where such craft excel

As recycling of Goliaths
Prolonging their grip
On the pinnacle of power while the masses
Experience power-cuts as daily anthems
Treading muddy road-stretches like pigs in mud-swims
Will there ever be change?

Will there ever be change
When those with sugar-tongues
Gain asylum while those in real need
Get rejected
On grounds of lack of proof
Unable to cook up tales of torments received at home
Like those gifted fast guys
Who've suddenly gained greener pastures
Denouncing under-bridges as erstwhile abodes
Sending home messages, cars and cash
Buying massive lands, building mansions, making families proud
Will there ever be change?

Ngalla Julius, 15 May 2016
Will there ever be change
When cold-blooded murderers coax
Mothers to murder their very babes
Unborn blood bundled up in bins full of factious fart
Of multi-billionaires whose reason is treason in seasons of siesta
Squandering in misappropriated motels with nymphets and nymphos
Neutralising dreams of a mission to mould a nation with

vision
The zombie loathes to face when in reunion with vampires
They smile in pain and grin in vain
To change the change they cannot change
Not so because they fear to do
But 'cos they pause to ponder and ask
Will there ever be change?

Ekpe Inyang, 16 May 2016
Will there ever be change
With daily cries of sorrow
As everyone feels so hollow
Huge crowds queueing out to borrow
Not sure to pay back tomorrow
Giant rats unable to burrow
Surely sick to the marrow
And pigs now cease to farrow
Feed supplies stopped by fellow
Sky boasting of no sparrow
Since nothing's there to swallow
Will there ever be change?

Charlotte DiangTitang, 14 May 2016
Will there ever be change
When your life lies in the hands of Doctor
When you either pay the price or die
When those trained to provide comfort
Turn to nagging you in your sickbed
When going abroad for treatment
Is the order of the day for leaders
Whose duty it is to develop home health sector
The poor left entirely at the mercy of

Those money-mongers in white
Demanding prices the poor can't pay
Will there ever be change?

Ekpe Inyang, 17 May 2016
Will there ever be change
When the lizard that nods its head
Upon its great achievements
Since no animal applauds good deeds
Gets castigated, branded arrogant
Mutely marginalised
Victimised, stagnated, glued back
Nailed to that spiteful rung
Eventually ostracised for
Daring to climb to that revered rung
Reserved for Goliaths of the land
Will there ever be change?

Patrick Tata, 15 May 2016
There will surely be change
When one Jerry Rawlins
Takes it up like a monster
Rampaging to spoil the present
Like God remaking
Disfigured clay bust to bring forth a better
One mad man mad
Enough to dare
The devil
Of all the hateful
Mounds of unpardonable errors
There will surely be change

Ekpe Inyang, 16 May 2016
Yes, there will surely be change
When personal hunts are cut
Increasing acts for general good
Answering all calls from numbers
Registered or unregistered
Known or unknown
Local or foreign
Opening the doors for all
Faces black or white
Known or unknown
When holding public keys
There will surely be change

Printed in the United States
By Bookmasters